Our Basic FREEDOMS

FREEDOM of SPEECH

JENNIFER MASON

Gareth Stevens
PUBLISHING

Please visit our website, www.garethstevens.com.
For a free color catalog of all our high-quality books,
call toll free 1-800-542-2595 or fax 1-877-542-2596.

Cataloging-in-Publication Data

Names: Mason, Jennifer.
Title: Freedom of speech / Jennifer Mason.
Description: New York : Gareth Stevens Publishing, 2017. | Series: Our basic freedoms | Includes index.
Identifiers: ISBN 9781482461084 (pbk.) | ISBN 9781482461862 (library bound) | ISBN 9781482461091 (6 pack)
Subjects: LCSH: Freedom of speech--United States--Juvenile literature.
Classification: LCC KF4772.M2853 2017 | DDC 342.7308'53--dc23

Published in 2017 by
Gareth Stevens Publishing
111 East 14th Street, Suite 349
New York, NY 10003

Developed and Produced by Focus Strategic Communications, Inc.
Project Manager: Adrianna Edwards
Editor: Ron Edwards
Layout and Composition: Laura Brady, Ruth Dwight
Copy Editors: Adrianna Edwards, Francine Geraci
Media Researchers: Maria DeCambra, Adrianna Edwards
Proofreader: Francine Geraci
Index: Ron Edwards

Photo Credits: Credit Abbreviations: LOC Library of Congress; NARA National Archives and Records
Administration; S Shutterstock; WC Wikimedia Commons. Position on the page: T: top, C: center, B: bottom, L:
left, R: right. Cover: C: Aaron Amat/S (photo); Jasemin90/S; R: AKaiser/S; Title Page: C: Aaron Amat/S (photo);
Jasemin90/S; R: AKaiser/S; 4: 360b/S; 5: Arindambanerjee/S; 6: Lara65/S; 7: Cheryl Casey/S; 8: Vkilikov/S; 9:
Everett Historical/S; 10: Daryl Lang/S; 11: chrisdorney/S; 12: LOC/LC-USZC4-4970; 14: Everett Historical/S;
15: LOC/LC-USZC4-5315; 16: Daderot/WC; 17 T: Everett Historical/S; 17 B: Lev Radin/S; 18: Everett - Art/S;
19: Everett Historical/S; 20: Billion Photos/S; 21: Everett Historical/S; 24: Billion Photos/S; 25: Evan El-Amin/S;
26: Steve Heap/S; 27: Rena Schild/S; 28: Sadik Gulec/S; 29: Cheryl Casey/S; 30: A katz/S; 31 T: Everett
Historical/S; 31 B: Everett Historical/S; 32: LOC/LC-F81-33172; 33: Jim Vallee/S; 34: NARA/194276; 36: Focus
Strategic Communications, Inc.; 37: Periscope/S; 38: LOC/LC-DIG-ppmsca-24360; 39: Everett Historical/S;
40: Dave O/WC; 41: Pavalena/S; 42: Stuart Miles/S; 43: Whytock/S; 44: Elena Kharichkina/S; 45: Lewis Tse Pui
Lung/S.

Printed in the United States of America
CPSIA compliance information: Batch CW17GS. For further information contact
Gareth Stevens, New York, New York at 1-800-542-2595.

CONTENTS

CHAPTER 1

THE BILL OF RIGHTS

CONSEQUENCES OF SPEAKING OUT

In some countries, expressing opinions, sharing information, writing articles, wearing clothes with particular symbols or slogans, and even making certain gestures can get people in a lot of trouble. That trouble can mean having to pay fines or serving time in jail. But those are minor consequences. In more severe instances, the "guilty" are simply abducted by government officials, never to be heard from again.

FREE-SPEECH VICTIMS

Aung San Suu Kyi spent 15 years under house arrest after trying to bring democratic government reforms such as free speech to Myanmar (Burma). From 1976 to 1983, more than 30,000 Argentine people were abducted after speaking out against their government. They never returned. They are known as *los desaparecidos*, or "the disappeared." In 2015, Lee Bo and four of his employees were abducted from the Hong Kong bookstore where they sold banned books. Evidence indicates the Chinese government may have played a role in their disappearance.

Aung San Suu Kyi was awarded the Nobel Peace Prize in 1991.

LIMITS OF FREE SPEECH

Speech that is not protected as a basic freedom comes with a heavy price tag.

Why do we as a nation allow and even encourage free speech when so many other countries suppress and restrict it as dangerous? Do we really allow anyone to say anything, or are there limits on this freedom? If so, are these limits justifiable? Are young people truly able to exercise free speech fully—even at school? Finally, can a list of amendments written more than 200 years ago protect our ultramodern tweets, posts, and chats?

The United States is one of only a few countries that vigorously protect a person's rights to speak or write freely.

EVERYONE HAS RIGHTS

The situation is different in the United States thanks to the Bill of Rights. The Bill of Rights generally refers to the first 10 amendments added to the Constitution in 1791. The ideas behind these additions stem from what were then new and emerging philosophies on "natural rights." Natural rights are thought to be inherent in all people. It does not matter what you look like, how old you are, or your gender. No matter where you come from, and no matter what, how, or whether you worship, you are forever endowed with natural rights simply because you are a member of the human race.

Natural rights do not hinge on your looks, your clothes, or your popularity. You possess them just as you possess the air in your lungs.

BILL OF RIGHTS CANS AND CANNOTS

If you look closely, you'll see that the Bill of Rights contains a lot of nos and shall nots. The Framers of the Constitution protected what people can do by telling the government what it cannot do.

Some amendments, like the Fourth Amendment, protect our property—such as our bodies, our homes, and our papers. The Sixth Amendment protects our right to a trial if we are accused of a crime and our right to have a lawyer. The Third Amendment does not allow the government to do things such as put soldiers in our homes. The Eighth Amendment prohibits the government from imposing excessive bail or fines or using cruel or unusual punishment.

THE EXACT RIGHT, EXACTLY RIGHT

"Congress shall make no law respecting an establishment of religion, or prohibiting the free exercise thereof; or abridging the freedom of speech, or of the press; or the right of the people peaceably to assemble, and to petition the Government for a redress of grievances."

That is the exact wording of the First Amendment. As you can see, this amendment grants a lot of freedoms besides speech. Or, more accurately, it restricts the government from hindering a person's religious practices or what a person has to say or wants to write. Additionally, the government cannot prevent anyone from assembling for meetings or protests, and it cannot forbid anyone from signing petitions or filing lawsuits.

NATURAL LAW AND NATURAL RIGHTS

The Founding Fathers believed in natural law and natural rights. Those are rights that no government can limit or deny. Compare that to legal rights, which are those given to individuals by the legal system of a state or other jurisdiction. Legal rights change whenever written laws change. Natural laws and natural rights are said to be **inalienable**, meaning they do not change and they cannot be given or taken away.

The back of the $2 bill features the Founding Fathers signing the Declaration of Independence. Assuming the bill was unpopular, the US Treasury stopped printing it in 1966. As it turned out, collectors were hoarding $2 bills because they were so rare. Even with $1.5 billion of these bills in circulation, they are still hard to find!

UNTOUCHABLE LIBERTIES

Because the government may not **abridge**, or shorten, what we say (speech) or write (press), we can express our thoughts, ideas, and opinions out loud or in writing.

"Abridge" is a term that means to shorten, as in an abridged novel, which is a shortened form of the book. However, another sense of the word is used in the US Constitution and Bill of Rights. There, the word means to weaken, diminish, or reduce rights. However, supporters of natural law believe that natural rights cannot be decreased or diluted by any law.

Fast Fact

JAMES MADISON AND THE BILL OF RIGHTS

James Madison brought some of the biggest ideas to the Constitutional Convention. Checks and balances, population-based representation, and a strong federal government were just three new notions Madison argued for. Initially, Madison opposed adding a Bill of Rights to the Constitution, which outlined what the government could do. He thought it was redundant to say what it could not do. But over time, he changed his mind and wrote the bulk of the first 10 amendments. Today, he is known as both the Father of the Constitution and the Father of the Bill of Rights.

ADDITIONAL FREEDOMS

Free speech means we are able to search the Internet for information and hear lectures in classrooms. What we see in movies and magazines and hear in music is also protected. We can disagree and debate with those who are in charge. The First Amendment also gives us the right to speak out, even when what we have to say is not popular.

Besides what we say or write, the First Amendment protects what we do. Carrying signs, wearing symbols on our T-shirts, and protesting are just a few examples of protected "speech acts," or actions that express ideas or have symbolic meaning.

And even if you don't find yourself at a noisy protest every day, safeguarding free speech affects young people in many complicated ways, especially at school. The clothes you can or cannot wear, the books you can or cannot read, and even the length of your hair—these are all free-speech issues that have been argued over in court.

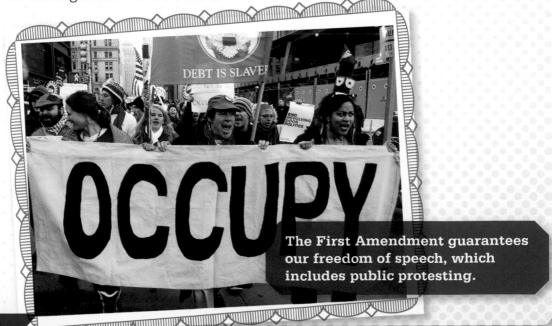

The First Amendment guarantees our freedom of speech, which includes public protesting.

STAMP OF DISAPPROVAL

But where did this urge to protect free speech come from? In the 1600s, Britain began establishing permanent **colonies** along the Atlantic coastline of the North American continent. For a long time, the colonies governed themselves. That arrangement changed after Britain fought and won the French and Indian War. Strapped with massive debts, the British government looked to the profitable colonies to help pay the bills.

Suddenly, American colonists were paying hefty taxes on everyday items such as molasses and newspapers. The tax on paper arose through the Stamp Act of 1765. It affected everything printed on paper—from legal documents to playing cards. The British government also ushered in a slew of other laws, which the colonists called the Intolerable Acts. The strict rules infringed upon colonial lifestyles and livelihoods by restricting trade, limiting the purchase of new land, and forcing colonists to share their homes with British soldiers. Rather than have their rights ignored and suppressed, the colonists declared their independence and went to war with England

Fast Fact

DAVID BOWIE

In the early 1960s, before he was a rock star, David Bowie formed the Society for the Prevention of Cruelty to Long-Haired Men. According to Bowie, men who had the courage to sport shaggy locks had a really tough time.

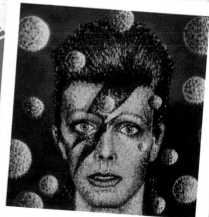

CHAPTER 2

LIMITED GOVERNMENT

NATURAL RIGHTS AND THE REVOLUTION

From 1775 to 1783, the American colonies fought Great Britain in order to win their independence as a nation unto themselves. In writing the Declaration of Independence in 1776 and fighting the brutal Revolutionary War against England, the American colonies embarked on a journey to become the first nation in the world to be established on the principles of natural rights.

The Battle of Bunker Hill, 1775, was one of the first battles of the American Revolution.

UPENDING THE POWER STRUCTURE

Natural rights upend the power structure that has shaped much of human civilization: **monarchs** or governments possess power and grant small portions of it as "rights" to the people they rule. In this formation, power trickles from the top down.

Around the 1600s, several English and Scottish writers and philosophers, including John Locke (1632–1704), speculated on a different power structure. Locke asserted that regardless of someone's class or nationality, all people were endowed with natural rights that they possessed simply because they were alive and human. In a sense, natural rights are like air—fundamental, essential, and naturally part of life.

Locke further argued that people did not give up their natural rights when they lived under the rule of a government. In fact, they entrusted their government to *protect* their rights. Power trickled from the bottom up, not the other way around.

NATURAL RIGHTS POWER STRUCTURE

Government

↑

People

JOHN LOCKE AND NATURAL RIGHTS

Around 1689, John Locke published *Two Treatises of Government*, where he spelled out his theories on natural rights. In the Second Treatise, Locke declared, "It is evident that all human beings—as creatures belonging to the same species and rank and born indiscriminately with all the same natural advantages and faculties—are equal amongst themselves."

EUROPEAN INFLUENCE

Like seeds on the wind, notions of natural rights spread from Europe to the American colonies and took root. Many of the **charters** establishing colonies included protections for natural rights. Locke's theories were echoed in the language Thomas Jefferson and the other Framers used to write the Declaration of Independence and the Constitution.

WARS AND PIECES

After the Revolutionary War, life was good. A ragtag gang of 13 misfit colonies had defeated one of the world's most powerful nations. Each colony became a sovereign state, able to make its own laws. Essentially, the states acted like mini-countries that agreed to "**confederate**," or be a league of friends. A Continental Congress tried to preside over the disunity of the squabbling states and would make sure everyone cooperated.

Fast Fact

JOIN OR DIE

Is it any wonder that a man who used keys and kites to capture lightning would draw a shocking political cartoon? In 1754, Benjamin Franklin first printed this drawing of a severed snake in his *Pennsylvania Gazette* newspaper. He hoped to spur the colonies to unite behind Britain in their battle against the French and Native American allies over control of the vast lands beyond the Appalachian Mountains. Two decades later, other newspapers used the iconic image to drive the colonists away from British control. Although Franklin opposed this use, the message was clear: if all the colonies did not join the revolution together, they would certainly all perish together.

THE UN-UNITED STATES OF AMERICA

About 10 years after the Declaration of Independence, the "united" states were in crisis. One state thought another was trying to overpower it. This state called that one some not-so-nice names. On top of it all, the new nation was financially strapped. The Continental Congress had no power to collect taxes and pay its bills. Finally, the new nation had no provisions in place for protection. The states had no way to fend off a foreign attack. In May 1787, delegates from the states convened at a Constitutional Convention to address the flaws of this new governmental system. After 4 months of work—in the summer, without air conditioning—they emerged with four sheets of parchment on which were jotted the United States Constitution.

The US Constitution was signed at the Constitutional Convention of 1787 in Philadelphia.

ALEXANDER HAMILTON

Alexander Hamilton was not only a driving force behind the formation of a Constitutional Convention, but he also had a brilliant mind geared to simplifying complicated systems, such as forming new nations.

Alexander Hamilton is on the face of the $10 bill.

Fast Fact

HAMILTON: AN AMERICAN MUSICAL

Alexander Hamilton's integral role in shaping the new nation is portrayed in the Broadway musical, *Hamilton: An American Musical*. **Lin-Manuel Miranda (pictured here) wrote and starred in this smash hit. The photo of Alexander Hamilton on the $10 bill was scheduled to be replaced in 2020. However, because of the popularity of the musical, Hamilton will remain on the bill.**

THE GAME PLAN

The Constitution established a central, or federal, government under which all the states united, forming an indivisible union. The Constitution also laid out the structure of the federal government, with plenty of ways to limit its powers.

Despite all the checks and balances of power, many states refused to **ratify**, or approve, the Constitution until it included clauses protecting the natural rights of citizens. Once the delegates of the Constitutional Convention agreed to attach a Bill of Rights, ratification came easily.

Fast Fact

★ ★ ★ ★
MADISON AS GAME MASTER

Like the game master of a role-playing game, James Madison (shown here) arrived at the Constitutional Convention with a blueprint for a federal government already mapped out. He designed a government made of three branches—executive, legislative, and judicial. Each branch had the power to check the powers of the other branches.

FOUNDING FATHERS AND FRAMERS

Of the 70 delegates chosen to attend the Constitutional Convention, only 55 arrived for the brutal task of hammering out the rules of the new nation, debating potential snags while scratching out and scribbling the wording in clearer phrases. These delegates are commonly known as the Framers of the Constitution. Thomas Jefferson, John Adams, John Jay, and several others are considered Founding Fathers because they brought about the war that, in turn, brought about the new nation. After the war, several Founding Fathers—George Washington, James Madison, Alexander Hamilton, and Benjamin Franklin, to name a few—went on to serve as Framers in the battle that was the Constitutional Convention.

Fast Fact

FRAMER OR FATHER?

What's the difference between a Founding Father and a Framer? Founders include the leaders and agitators who brought about and fought the Revolutionary War. Framers were those who debated and drafted the blueprint documents such as the Constitution. Thus, Founders and Framers can be divided into the Fighters and the Writers. George Washington (pictured here) was both a Founding Father and a Framer.

CHAPTER 3

INTERPRETING RIGHTS

LOST FOR WORDS

Besides its revolutionary stance on freedoms, the US Constitution is a remarkable document because it is so short. Without the Bill of Rights, the whole text totals 4,543 words—including the signatures! Not bad for a document establishing a radically new form of government that the world had never seen before! Compare that to the 50,000 words in Major League Baseball's official rulebook!

But even before the ink on the parchment had dried, arguments broke out over the meanings of many of the Constitution's words.

Fast Fact

PARCHMENT PAPER

The Declaration of Independence, the Constitution, and the Bill of Rights were all written on parchment. Jacob Shallus, who was known for his excellent penmanship, copied the wording of the Constitution onto parchment. Although it is often called "paper," parchment is actually animal skin that has been cleaned and dried. The most common source was calfskin. Today, most paper is made from wood pulp.

WHO ARE "PEOPLE"?

Perhaps the most contested words might be "people" and "persons." Theoretically, all "people" were endowed with natural rights. In practice, however, the only people who really got to enjoy those rights were white men, and usually only those who owned property. Women and black slaves were not considered full "people." They were thought of as lesser beings—less able and less smart.

In the months and years after the Civil War (1861–1865), the Thirteenth, Fourteenth, and Fifteenth Amendments to the Constitution expanded the interpretation of "people" to include former slaves. By 1920, the Nineteenth Amendment determined that women were also "people" who were entitled to the right to vote.

Fast Fact

SUFFRAGISTS

In 1878, Congress considered adding an amendment to the Constitution that would give women the right to vote, also known as **suffrage**. Besides voting, women were not allowed to earn wages, own property, study at universities, or play sports. Women's rights activists, called suffragists, picketed, paraded, filed lawsuits, and more! By 1920, thanks to tireless efforts of activists such as Elizabeth Cady Stanton, Lucretia Mott, and Susan B. Anthony, the Nineteenth Amendment guaranteed all American women the right to vote.

THE ROLE OF COURTS

Whenever disputes erupt over the exact meaning of the words in the Constitution, the Supreme Court can choose to step in to deliver an exact interpretation.

In general, courts are where people go when they have a disagreement about what laws mean and whether laws were broken. Some courts are designed to handle very specific legal matters such as taxes, bankruptcy, or family matters like divorce. Others, including state, district, and municipal courts, are limited by their jurisdiction, or the reach of their legal power. For instance, state courts deal only with state laws.

TYPES OF COURTS

Some courts hear trials. Others hear **appeals**. Trial courts are a lot like what you might see in movies, where the two arguing sides—the prosecution/plaintiff and the defense—present evidence to support their side of the argument, or "case," before a judge and jury who deliver a decision, or "ruling."

If either the prosecution/plaintiff or the defense does not agree with that decision, they can appeal it. That means they can ask another court to review the decision to see if a mistake was made.

SUPREME COURT CHOOSES CAREFULLY!

Each year, between 7,000 and 8,000 cases are submitted to the US Supreme Court, but of those, usually only about 80 are heard. Generally, the Court tries to pick cases that will have the broadest impact across the country. Almost all cases heard by the Court are appeals from lower courts, whether federal or state.

THE US FEDERAL COURT SYSTEM

US Supreme Court

US Appeals Courts

US District Courts

THE STATE COURT SYSTEM

State Supreme Courts

State Appeals Courts

State District Courts

HOW THE SUPREME COURT WORKS

The US Supreme Court is, as its name implies, the highest court in the land. It hears appeals from lower courts, which is why it is known as an appellate court. Not only that, it is the supreme appellate court of the entire country. Once the Supreme Court makes a decision, no other court can overturn that decision.

The nine judges serving on the Supreme Court are called justices. The one justice appointed to be the leader of the court is called the Chief Justice. Once the Supreme Court has decided to hear a case, the justices receive briefs from the plaintiffs and the defense. Briefs are written arguments for either side of the case. Finally, the lawyers for both sides present oral arguments.

Fast Fact

GAVEL

Think "courtroom" and you're likely to conjure the image of a judge calling for order in the court and banging that small mallet known as a gavel. Gavels date back to the medieval era, but they are hardly, if ever, used in real courtrooms today.

THE SUPREME COURT IN ACTION

The oral arguments are open to the public and can be thrilling (and amusing) to watch as the justices pepper the lawyers with puzzling, sometimes snarky, questions.

Fast Fact
ANTONIN SCALIA

Antonin Scalia died in February 2016 at the age of 79. He is seen in a 2007 oil painting, displayed at his funeral in the Great Hall of the Supreme Court. Scalia was appointed to the Supreme Court in 1986 by Ronald Reagan and served for nearly 30 years (10,732 days) as Supreme Court justice. But he ranks only number 15 by length of term of justices. In first place is William O. Douglas, who served 13,358 days between 1939 and 1975. Scalia was known as a defender of executive power (even when he disagreed with the president's opinion). However, at the same time, he defended states' rights against federal powers.

DECISIONS AND DISSENTS

After oral arguments, the justices take their time to issue a decision. They can spend weeks or months reviewing all the information in a case. When the justices are ready, they each cast a vote. The side with the most votes wins the appeal.

Once the votes are cast, the Supreme Court must write up its opinion. Usually, the Chief Justice selects a justice to write the opinion. When the ruling is very controversial or complicated, the Chief Justice often writes the opinion. That involves clearly explaining how and why the Court came to its decision—how it interpreted the language of the Constitution, what logic it used, and what **precedents** it followed. Following precedent means that the justices look back on previous Supreme Court decisions and use those as a guide. Finally, the justices who disagree with the opinion can also write **dissents**.

The US Supreme Court in Washington, DC, was completed in 1935. It is located on the block just east of the US Capitol.

THE SUPREME COURT AND FREE SPEECH

Following this process throughout many decades and hundreds of cases, the Supreme Court has tried to determine precisely what speech is and just how free it is. What if hardly anyone agrees with what you have to say? And whether you put your ideas in a song or on a sign, what if they deeply hurt someone else's feelings?

Fast Fact

CONTROVERSIAL DECISIONS

On June 26, 2015, the US Supreme Court established an all-new **civil right** across all 50 states when it ruled in favor of same-sex marriages. Joyous crowds flooded the plaza outside the Court, and rainbow lights illuminated the White House. The 5–4 decision came at a time when at least one-third of Americans did not support gay marriage.

CHAPTER 4

THE FIRST AMENDMENT

FREE SPEECH OR HARASSMENT?

The war in Iraq, or Operation Iraqi Freedom, was launched in 2003. The United States led a coalition of other nations bent on toppling the corrupt leader Saddam Hussein. He was quickly captured in December 2003, and tried, convicted, and executed in 2006. The United States succeeded within a few months, but the war developed into many civil wars. They rage to this day.

Lance Corporal Matthew Snyder was 20 years old when he died in a Humvee rollover accident in Iraq in 2006. Although he was not killed in combat, Corporal Snyder still joined the more than 4,400 US military deaths in the war in Iraq.

His grieving family planned a peaceful, honorable funeral to commemorate Matthew's life and service. Outside the cemetery, they encountered a raucous, seething horde of protesters from the Westboro Baptist Church.

US soldiers stand guard at a checkpoint on January 26, 2007, in Maxmur, Iraq.

THE FREE WORD OF GOD

The Westboro Baptists believed that Matthew's death—and every death accumulated in the Afghan and Iraqi wars—was a form of divine punishment. To express this idea, they gathered at the funerals of servicemen and servicewomen around the country wearing T-shirts and carrying signs plastered with disturbing **epithets**, such as "God blew up the troops" and "Thank God for dead soldiers." They shouted at Matthew's family and heckled all the mourners.

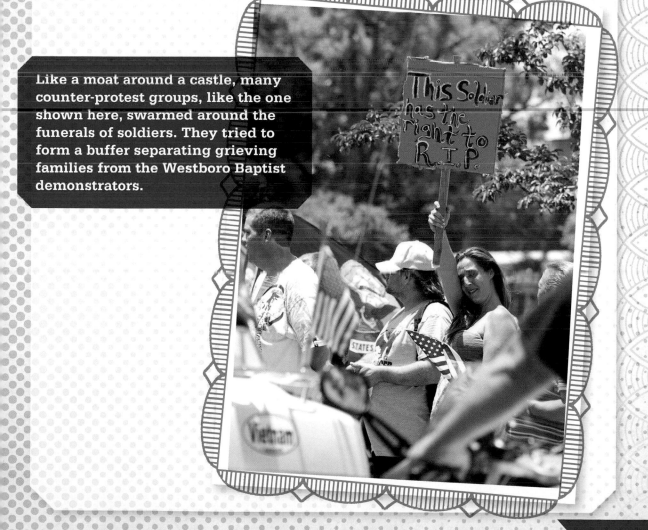

Like a moat around a castle, many counter-protest groups, like the one shown here, swarmed around the funerals of soldiers. They tried to form a buffer separating grieving families from the Westboro Baptist demonstrators.

SNYDER V. PHELPS

When Matthew's family sued, the Westboro Baptist Church argued that their protests were protected as free speech. The case wound up in the Supreme Court. In 2011, eight justices ruled in favor of the church's freedom of speech—what the protesters yelled, or put on signs or on their shirts, was protected by the First Amendment. It didn't matter if their speech was "distasteful and repugnant."

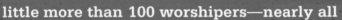

WESTBORO BAPTIST CHURCH

Fred Phelps started the Westboro Baptist Church (WBC) in Topeka, Kansas, in 1955. Since then, the congregation has grown to a little more than 100 worshipers—nearly all members of the Phelps family. The church first made headlines in 1998 when it demonstrated at the funeral of Matthew Shepard, a young gay man who was beaten and tortured to death. Shepard's murder kicked off national action to prevent hate crimes. Nonetheless, the WBC went on to demonstrate and spread hate speech at the funerals of celebrities and soldiers, and at the graves of small children who died in a tragic bus wreck. They even appeared in front of Ground Zero during memorial services on the thirteenth anniversary of the World Trade Center attack with signs praising the attack.

UNPOPULAR SUPREME COURT RULINGS

The *Snyder v. Phelps* case is not the only time the Supreme Court allowed unpopular ideas to be freely expressed. The Court ruled that the Ku Klux Klan had a right to voice its racist and hostile views as long as its members did not incite "lawless action." Similarly, Americans supporting the Nazi regime in Germany were allowed to march and demonstrate in Jewish neighborhoods.

The Ku Klux Klan (KKK) was founded in the South after the end of the Civil War. What started out as late-night shenanigans intended to frighten newly freed slaves quickly morphed into outright terrorism. By the 1920s, the KKK swelled to over 3 million members! In 1925, 40,000 robed and hooded "klansmen" paraded through Washington, DC.

Fast Fact

JUSTICE LOUIS BRANDEIS

Louis Brandeis was appointed to the US Supreme Court by Woodrow Wilson in 1916. He was the first Jewish justice to serve on the nation's highest court. Brandeis had practiced law in Boston, Massachusetts, where he became known as "the people's lawyer." He fought against big corporations, vigorously defending people's freedom of speech. In May 1927, he said: "When we are confronted with speech we don't agree with, the remedy to be applied is more speech . . . not enforced silence."

LIMITS OF FREE SPEECH

Even though it seems the Supreme Court gives the green light to just about any kind of speech, there have been times when it stripped that right away. For instance, the Supreme Court has ruled that free speech does not protect obscenity. Additionally, the Court has found that speech is not protected when it presents a "clear and present" danger. This means that you can't falsely shout "Fire!" in a crowded place because the resulting panic could endanger everyone scrambling for safety.

Fast Fact

OLIVER WENDELL HOLMES

Oliver Wendell Holmes was one of the great defenders of free speech. He composed one of his most famous decisions in the **landmark** case *Schenck v. United States* (1919). Charles Schenk distributed pamphlets telling men not to enlist as soldiers during World War I, violating the Espionage Act of 1917. Schenck argued that his pamphlets were protected free speech, but the Supreme Court ruled unanimously against him. In his opinion for the Court, Holmes concluded that during wartime, Schenck's writing was just like someone falsely shouting, "Fire!" in a crowded theater. Essentially, keeping men from enlisting as soldiers during a war put the nation in grave danger.

CONTROVERSIAL SYMBOLS

With slogans, picket signs, white robes, and swastikas, it is much easier to recognize the controversies ignited through the expression of ideas. But what about silent statements that come without printed or spoken words of any kind? And what about when those silent expressions are carried out by children instead of adults?

Fast Fact

★ ★ ★
SWASTIKA

Today, the hooked cross symbol, or swastika, conjures dreaded memories of Adolf Hitler and the Holocaust in Germany during World War II, when over 6 million Jewish people and millions of others were killed by the Nazis. But the swastika was not always an icon for hate-driven death and destruction—quite the opposite! Archaeologists believe the symbol dates back at least 5,000 years and represents the movement of the sun through the sky. It is a sacred motif found in many Hindu and Buddhist temples. In ancient Sanskrit, *svastika* means "good fortune" or "well-being."

CHAPTER 5

STUDENT RIGHTS

SOCIAL CHANGE

The 1960s marked a time of massive upheaval and social change in America. Minorities protested across the country, demanding the rights otherwise withheld from them. President John F. Kennedy and civil rights leader Martin Luther King Jr. were both assassinated.

Kennedy adopted vigorous action to guarantee civil rights for all. Theories and conspiracies abound for the reason behind his murder, but it is possible his stance on civil rights may have been a factor. In contrast, Martin Luther King's murder leaves little room for speculation. He was targeted not only because he was black, but also because he was the leader of the Civil Rights Movement in America at the time. Through the freedom of speech, King harnessed the power of words to preach nonviolent resistance against **segregation** and discrimination.

Civil rights leaders, including Martin Luther King Jr. (third from left), meet with President John F. Kennedy (center) in the Oval Office of the White House after the March on Washington, DC, in August 1963.

VIETNAM WAR

When America went to war with Vietnam, young people broke out in huge protests and defied the draft that required them to fight. Besides the draft, young people defied all kinds of systems and figures of authority, especially at school. When the Supreme Court weighed in, it got supremely tangled in a jungle gym of complex issues.

Fast Fact

PROTEST ANTHEM

In 1966, when the city of Los Angeles passed a 10 p.m. curfew, youngsters quickly gathered in protest to defend their civil rights. The ensuing riots and clashes with the police inspired Steven Stills of the band Buffalo Springfield to write the song, "For What It's Worth." The song became an anthem for the youth movement sweeping across America. "It's time we stop, hey, what's that sound? / Everybody look what's going down."

UP IN ARMS

In 1965, in the midst of these chaotic times, four students went to their public elementary and high schools in Iowa wearing black armbands—a silent, symbolic protest of the Vietnam War. Even so, this seemingly small act kicked off a huge debate about the rights of young people and where those rights could be expressed.

TINKER V. DES MOINES SCHOOL DISTRICT

At home, John Tinker (15), Mary Beth Tinker (13), their 11-year-old sister Hope, and their close friend Christopher Eckhardt agreed to wear the armbands to school. The principal did not mind that they were expressing their opinions about the war, but he was worried that it could cause disruptions. He told the children to remove the armbands or be suspended.

The students refused to take off the armbands and later sued the school for violating their right to free speech. In a 7–2 decision, the Supreme Court ruled in favor of the Tinkers' armbands as a protected speech act. In his opinion for the court, Justice Abe Fortas wrote, "It can hardly be argued that either students or teachers shed their constitutional right to freedom of speech or expression at the schoolhouse gate."

The Tinkers and Eckhardt wore black armbands similar to this to protest the Vietnam War.

STUDENT RIGHTS (OR WRONGS) ON CAMPUS

Tinker v. Des Moines School District is a landmark case for several reasons. First, the highest court in the country asserted that students possessed rights, especially free speech, even at schools. Many people thought the *Tinker* ruling merely opened the floodgates for disobedience on campus.

Plenty of schoolhouse cases followed. For example, in *Hazelwood School District v. Kuhlmeier* (1988), the Court ruled that schools could censor material printed in a student newspaper. Besides **censorship**, the Court was called in to decide on whether boys could have long hair—especially when the length of hair was intended as a symbolic form of protest—and whether contentious books could be removed from school libraries.

Students do not enjoy freedom of speech as outlined in the First Amendment when they write for a school-sponsored publication.

WAR PROTESTS ESCALATE

Started in 1955, the Vietnam War spiraled on for nearly 2 decades, until President Richard Nixon ordered the withdrawal of US forces in 1973. The North Vietnamese conquered the South in 1975. Casualties were heavy, with some estimates running over 1 million people. The war cost the United States the lives of nearly 60,000 soldiers. The battles and brutalities inflicted on all sides exceeded the horrors of most nightmares. Antiwar protests spread across the country. Many included children and young people like the Tinkers who wanted the conflict to end.

Students across the country protested against US involvement in the Vietnam War. Here, protesters march outside the White House in Washington, DC, in 1968.

BOOK BURNINGS

Book burnings are one of the most extreme forms of free-speech suppression. Destroying books by feeding them to a blazing fire is not uncommon in human history. Medieval Vikings and, later, French Enlightenment revolutionaries burned entire libraries. However, those acts were generally considered vandalism—more the destruction of property than of ideas.

Elsewhere in history, **tyrants** and other extremists burned the books and writings that undermined their control or contradicted their beliefs. Along these lines, pro-Nazi student groups perpetrated one of the most notorious book burnings of the modern era. In May 1933, upwards of 25,000 books harboring supposedly "un-German" ideologies fueled bonfires across Germany.

The German Student Association of Nazi Germany referred to its 1933 book burning as a *Säuberung*, or "cleansing."

Fast Fact

HARRY POTTER

J. K. Rowling's Harry Potter series sold more than 450 million copies in 73 languages between 1997 and 2013. However, the series is not beloved by all. Some critics believe the books promote witchcraft or subversive political ideas. For nearly a decade, the Harry Potter series reigned as the most frequently banned books, which meant that many libraries either could not or would not put the books on their shelves.

CHAPTER 6

CONCLUSION

MIXED MESSAGES

Morse v. Frederick (2007) remains one of the Supreme Court's last **verdicts**—and one of its most muddled decisions—regarding young people's freedom of speech.

In 2002, the city of Juneau, Alaska, received some very exciting news: the Olympic Torch was going to travel through town on its circuit around the world. Several teachers at the public high school planned to take their students out of the classroom to watch the celebratory procession pass right in front of their school.

Fast Fact

OLYMPIC TORCH RELAY

According to ancient Greek myth, the man Prometheus stole fire from the gods and gave it to humankind. Not surprisingly, the flaming torch became a symbol for great human achievement. Today's greatest athletes compete in the modern Olympic Games. A few months before the games begin, the torch is lit in Olympia, Greece, and carried on a Promethean route around the world.

Juneau is located in southern Alaska, near the Canadian border.

PRANKSTERS

Before the parade reached the school, several students crossed to the opposite side of the street. Finally, the athletes marched by with the torch ablaze. News vans, photographers, and reporters followed along, recording everything and everyone. Suddenly, the students across the street unraveled a huge 14-foot banner with a message praising drug use.

The school principal, Deborah Morse, quickly removed the banner and rounded up the pranksters. She soon learned that the person behind the stunt was a student named Joe Frederick. Morse promptly suspended him from school.

TINKERING WITH THE OUTCOME

Two lower courts wrangled with the drug banner. One court sided with Frederick, the other with Principal Morse. The case landed in the Supreme Court in 2006. Drawing on precedent, the justices naturally looked back on *Tinker v. Des Moines*. Was Frederick's banner just like the armbands? Was it a protected speech act?

In a razor-close 5–4 decision, the Court determined that Frederick's First Amendment rights were not violated. Chief Justice Roberts wrote the opinion for the Court. However, in a strange turn of events, the justices who voted with him also wrote their own opinions about why they voted the way they did. They announced that they disagreed with certain parts of Chief Justice Roberts's opinion. In effect, they sort of agreed the ruling was sort of right and sort of wrong. Likewise, the justices who disagreed with the court opinion wrote conflicting dissents. That is, everyone disagreed with the ruling, but they each disagreed for different reasons.

Sometimes, when the issue facing the Supreme Court is particularly controversial, the best the justices can do is agree to disagree.

ARMBANDS VERSUS BANNERS

Why were the Tinkers and Eckhardt protected when Frederick was not? According to Chief Justice Roberts's opinion for the Court, the Tinkers' armbands were a symbol of opposition to a war, not to the school or any of its policies. Frederick testified that he displayed the banner not because he disagreed with the Olympics, but rather, to see how his school would react. Therefore, Roberts reasoned, Frederick's banner was intended to clash with the school's anti-drug policy.

DRUG-FREE SCHOOLS

Since 1986, schools in the United States are required by law to be drug-free zones. Under the Safe and Drug-Free Schools and Communities Act, schools initiated many anti-drug programs intended to educate young people about the health risks and criminal dangers commonly associated with drug abuse. The drug-free zone includes school buses on their routes through towns and cities!

ONLINE ON THE LINE

With data-packed smartphones in our pockets, our ideas travel with us, like digital armbands and banners. At present, the lower courts are churning with complicated disputes over speech that begins in e-mails, blogs, tweets, and texts and then winds up in unprotected places. What precedent will the courts use from the tangled *Morse v. Frederick* decision? How will the law treat a student who freely expresses an online idea at home, but then brings that idea to school on his phone, laptop, or tablet? Will this digital speech be protected, or will it be squelched?

Will a person's freedom of speech be protected in online communication?

In September 2014, young people flooded around Hong Kong's government headquarters, peacefully protesting for more free speech protections online. The demonstrators raised their glowing smartphones into the air, forming a bright blue "glocean."

SILENT NO MORE

The impulse to silence speech in its many forms reaches around the world and all the way back through human history. Perhaps the intent is to prevent anarchy, social disorder, blasphemy, and obscenity. Or maybe it's just to avoid bothersome opinions. And while the Supreme Court's rulings on free speech are not always clear or consistent, one thing is: words have power—a power worth protecting.

GLOSSARY

abridge — to make shorter, as in "abridged books"

appeal — a request for help

censorship — the act of removing unfavorable words, pictures, or ideas

charters — official documents that explain rights or duties

civil rights — rights guaranteed to all citizens

colonies — places where a group of people are sent to settle

confederate — to be united in a league; to be allies

dissent — to disagree with others; an opposing decision

epithet — a word or phrase that accurately or sometimes cruelly describes a person or thing, as in "man's best friend" to describe dogs, or "Honest Abe" to describe President Lincoln

inalienable — impossible to take away or give up

landmark — an event that marks an important change

monarchs — rulers, such as kings, queens, or emperors, who control a kingdom or empire

precedent — an example or rule to be followed in the future

ratify — to give legal or official approval

segregation — the practice of separating people into groups, usually based on race or class

suffrage — the right to vote

tyrant — a ruler without any limits on power who acts unfairly

verdict — the decision of a judge or jury

FURTHER INFORMATION

Books

Cahill, Bryon. *Freedom of Speech and Expression*. South Egremont, MA: Red Chair Press, 2014.

Hennessey, Jonathan, and Aaron McConnell. *The Gettysburg Address: A Graphic Adaptation*. New York: HarperCollins, 2013.

Sheinkin, Steve. *The Port Chicago 50: Disaster, Mutiny, and the Fight for Civil Rights*. New York: Roaring Brook Press, 2014.

Online

Bill of Rights Institute
www.billofrightsinstitute.org/

Center for Civic Education
www.civiced.org/

C-SPAN Classroom
www.c-spanclassroom.org/

Library of Congress
www.loc.gov/families/

National Archives
www.archives.gov/

Oyez Project at IIT Chicago-Kent College of Law
www.oyez.org/

INDEX